*With the sword of my will, I carve for myself a throne in the realm of the Spirit, which I shall ascend.*

# THOUGHTS FOR ASPIRANTS

" WISDOM is not a matter of study, but a matter of living."

" Each must discover his own way in life, and that way lies in his heart. Let him delve deeply into the depths of his being; his true center is not far from there."

These are just two of the many inspirational and profound ideas embodied in this small work, compiled from the writings of N. Sri Ram of India, fifth international President of The Theosophical Society. Each beautiful statement contains a wealth of meaning to be pondered upon in one's mind and heart.

This is an abridgment of the larger edition and is published in a smaller pocket size as part of the Quest Miniature series.

# Thoughts
## For Aspirants

Compiled from Notes and Writings
of

## N. Sri Ram

This publication made possible with
the assistance of the Kern Foundation

The Theosophical Publishing House
Wheaton, Ill. U.S.A.
Madras, India/London, England

©1972 by the Theosophical
Publishing House. All Rights Reserved

First published 1950. First Quest Miniature
Edition 1972
Second Q.M. Printing 1989

Published by the Theosophical Publishing
House, a department of the Theosophical
Society in America, Wheaton, Illinois
by arrangement with the Theosophical
Publishing House, Madras, India

ISBN: 0-8356-0431-4

Printed in the United States of America

*Cover design by*
Jane A. Evans & Madhu

# CONTENTS

vi

# I

## SELF-REALIZATION

THE whole process of evolution, for the Spirit, is an awakening to the truths, and the means of implementation of those truths, that are eternally present in itself. What was implicit has to become explicit.

To know the not-Self in one's nature is the pathway to knowledge of the Self.

When you discover for yourself, however dimly, that you are rooted in something that is infinitely vast and potential, you have found the soil wherein you grow unconsciously into a most wonderful tree, the tree of life blended with knowledge.

Long not for anything which will give a greater conceit of self, but for a truer realization of that selfless Self which is the center and origin of every being.

Man has to discover for himself that what he thinks as being himself, what he calls " myself," is an illusion, a *maya*, which is but a cloak of many colors like those that appear on a bubble in the sunlight.

Since all truths pertaining to oneself are realizations in oneself, they must be part of ourselves, our realized being.

We have to achieve the true and perfect expression of that which is inmost in ourselves—which is the release of ourselves from our prison-house.

The way of Self-Realization, as shown in the ancient books, is the way of repudiation, a withdrawal from all things external to the Self.

Man begins to unfold that which he eternally is only through reliance on himself. The uniqueness that is each individual being is the true separation of self from Self, of the individual center from the universal Manas.

Man is more than his environment. It is from the innate quality of the Spirit in him, his inner storehouse, that he draws those ideas, his intuitions, which unify his perceptions of the external world instantaneously with a value which is qualitative and not quantitative, and which he embodies in the works of his culture—those achievements which belong not only to one particular time but to all times, and mark the path of his upward progress.

You can never realize anything with the mind, unless you have already realized it intuitively in a passive state. What is first known within, in the region that to us is dark, is later brought into light.

He who becomes the master of himself can become master over all that is related to himself. Self-mastery implies self-knowledge and that self-sufficiency which is only in love.

Remember that the whole sense of one's importance is merely an evaluation of self by self.

It is only when man realizes that there is in himself no center around which he can build permanently, that he will begin to seek and can find that true center, which is everywhere and nowhere.

Know for yourself the way along which you should go—do not depend upon others.

It is I alone who frame on those other lips the words that may hurt me.

Our growth consists not merely in an increase of ideas, but also in a capacity to feel in a million and one ways.

The Alone is the unity, and the " flight of the alone to the Alone " is a process of realization, which is achieved in perfect stillness. When you are alone in the pure spiritual sense, which is a withdrawal from all that in yourself has been moulded from without, you find yourself in that other Alone which is the uncreated Unity.

Each must discover the heavenliness, the expanding universe of his own being.

Before we can transcend limitations, whether in our own nature or in the circumstances around us, we must try to understand what it is that they are meant to teach.

Each must discover his own way in life, and that way lies in his heart. Let him delve deeply into the depths of his being; his true center is not far from there.

Every premature withdrawal from the battle of life, merely because it involves stress and strain which we think is too much for us, fails to fulfil the object with which we have entered that battle.

No one can gain a true knowledge of himself without facing adversity and overcoming difficulties. But in developing the dynamism to overcome, there must be naught of the spirit of aggression or aggrandisement.

The moment we are aware of a hindrance in our nature to that fulfilment which all Life unconsciously seeks, aware of it as a fetter upon ourselves, that moment we are on the way to its abolition.

It is the direction of our progress that matters—not where we stand at present.

I am no more—and no less—than a law of Life's expression.

I struggle with myself; I cannot escape from myself; let me re-shape myself in terms of that which is Universal.

No individual can ultimately fail. The Divinity which descends into humanity is bound to regain its original state.

It is only when there is self-knowledge, resulting in perfect control over and unification of ourselves, that we can offer our will to be part of the one Spiritual Will, which in reality is in ourselves and *is* ourselves.

## II

## WILL

THERE is nothing in the whole of Nature except the Will of the Divine. It is the Will of the one Center of every circle of life.

Will is not the focusing of diverse energies at a superficial point, but the focusing of yourself at your center. Since that center has no space or location, its consciousness can act at any point.

What we call "willing" is often but an inflation of ourselves, attended by a hardening.

Desire is but will inverted. It is a pull of matter, instead of the free movement of the Spirit.

Action and understanding are unified in the Will. An act of will that does not carry within itself understanding is no true will at all.

In the Spiritual Will there is no coercion of an unwilling self, for the Will is one and moves as a whole.

True self-determination takes its rise from a dimensionless point. It is not to be confused with any personal reaction. To arise and take place, it needs a heart and mind emptied of all predilections and prejudices.

The will is a product of integrity, not a
child of contradictions.

*※*

To will spiritually, originally and funda-
mentally; ever to give that will vibrant, creative
and multiplying expression; let that be our
constant aim.

*※*

Self-initiative is will in the true sense.

*※*

The true will never strains; it is born in
silence. It includes both thought and feeling.
It is immovable by anything external to itself.
When I have no will of my own, I can act with
the strongest will in the world. When I know
that the one Will is in all, all conflict is abolished.

*※*

The will must move on a path of its own, self-isolated. Obstacles may check action, but they cannot check the will behind the possible action.

We must bring the body, emotions and mind into the state of a completely obedient and flexible instrument of the Spiritual Will, in which there is only motion, no obstinacy, no insistence.

The will of God is in all things. But the self-will of man obscures it, as a plate might obscure the distant sun, while man and God are apart.

Will is not obstinacy, not autocracy, but self-direction.

To will the perfect end is also to will the means, for perfection starts from now. In the one true Will, end and means are unified.

We must will to dare all and challenge everything, be bursting with initiative, yet remain within the bounds of an eternal harmony and synthesis.

Let your courage mount with difficulties. There would be no will if there were no resistance.

Determine to solve all problems created by the play of opposites and overcome all difficulties; will to attempt any precipice or fall into any abyss, in the unshaken conviction that

while every vesture of manifestation may be
splintered into its atoms, the invincible, eternal
You will remain and arise.

When once the true Will is awakened, it
can never again be put to sleep. When once the
connection is formed between the apex of a
man's true nature and its foundation in the
realm of matter, that connection cannot,
ordinarily, cease to exist. It is by the power
of the Ātman, the Godhead within, that he
achieves what would otherwise be a seeming
miracle.

## II

## TRUTH

WHAT is Truth? Is it an object of knowledge; an object of love and of the knowledge which is at the fountain-head of love? Or does it consist, even more than these, in a universal self-identification, giving rise to the incorporation of the essence of every other being in oneself, and the living of a life that is at each point a perfect consummation of oneself? In this last view, Truth is a becoming but with a quality of finality, a progressive attainment yet a realization. Truth is Life in its highest, most evolved state, the fullest revelation of its essence.

Before we can receive in our hearts the Truth which springs from the deepest part of ourselves, we have to be prepared by a cleansing, a baptism, not merely with water but also with fire.

Truth is one and the same at all times, though it is infinite in its manifestation. But each must find it by the realization of it within himself. And he can realize it only as he seeks to embody it in his life, so that all he is and does becomes more and more beautiful each day.

All virtues are forms of Truth; each is an effect proceeding from the very nature of the thing.

The motion of the Spirit, its action, projects Truth from within, and speaks in accents of wisdom, using a language which is the very language of Truth.

All ideals are heaven-inspired dreams, visions of Truth, which resides in its fullness in the Divine or spiritual Self. When the ideal and the real are one, thought and life coincide.

✲

Every spritual Truth, being living, has a dynamism of its own, which translates it into action.

✲

The Truth which we seek must be the Truth of direct experience, in which the distinction between subject and object has ceased to exist. Only a disinterested search can result in Truth, for every form of self-interest will lead only to a creation which will serve that self-interest.

✲

Truth belongs to Life, as facts belong to form. When the essential nature of Life is perfectly expressed in the form with which it is clothed, the form becomes the form of Truth.

Truth leans neither to this side nor to that. It is balanced, impartial and just.

Truth is a " pathless land," because intuition is pathless.

Truth recedes into the background when the speaker about Truth is very much in the fore-ground.

A truth which does not emerge in the form of its appropriate expression is a truth which is devoid of power.

Truth, beauty and goodness stand or fall together. One test of Truth, therefore, is goodness; another is beauty.

Truth is intrinsic. What is intrinsic is important, whether in a grain of wood or the heart of a sage.

The Truth is within us, but we have to become aware of that Truth; it is involved in our being, and has to be evolved out of it, which evolution is as objective as it is subjective.

When Truth is the center of one's being and Love radiates therefrom, all things are comprehended and achieved, for the rays of Truth are then carried everywhere.

Truth is no one's property. It cannot be possessed, it belongs to no one, or rather, it belongs to everyone and everything.

Truth is infinite, and as we delve more deeply into it, we shall find yet greater depths, wider latitudes, and ever-new dimensions.

The Truth we seek must completely fill our being and pour through every expression of ourselves in thought, feeling and action.

What you are deep within yourself is the Truth of your being. What you seem and do must flow from that Truth and be patterned upon it.

Some day we will project the rays of the Truth within us, to which nothing is impenetrable, so that we shall know the nature of each thing as it is, see it in that clear light which reveals all its hidden riches.

Happy the man who can say: The self in me has vanished, and Truth has taken its place.

It is only when self has disappeared that the Truth which is in the heart of being, in the heart of each individual, can manifest itself in its purity, its essentialness and all its charm and beauty.

## IV

## WISDOM

WISDOM is an aspect of God, which shines through the creative Spirit. Hence, His Wisdom is in all things, in their being as well as their becoming, in each separate thing as well as in the totality.

In the light of God's Wisdom, all human knowledge is but ignorance.

Wisdom is not a question of learning facts with the mind; it can only be acquired through perfection of living.

Wisdom is a root-principle in man, which has to flower in right thought, right action and right living from every point of view.

He is the wise man who is able to distinguish between his limited wisdom and his unlimited ignorance.

There is no Wisdom without love. The heart of Love, embedded in knowledge, is transformed into Wisdom.

Wisdom implies knowledge of life, in addition to knowledge of form: a knowledge not only of particulars, but also of that which binds the particulars, the unity in them.

To discover the law of one's own being and live it is Wisdom.

To know ourselves, at least to the extent we are able to see ourselves, is the first step to Wisdom, and such knowledge will increasingly bring both clarity and charity.

Wisdom is not knowledge, but lies in the use we make of knowledge. It arises from knowledge guided by love. To use knowledge with goodness is to make it shine with a value which reflects Eternity in time.

We cannot separate one aspect of Wisdom from another, neither the philosophic from the scientific, nor the wisdom that is in the heart

from the wisdom that issues from the hands,
in other words, the ideal from the practical.

Wisdom shines with a dual quality of courage
and caution.

When Wisdom is absolute, the reason can
extend indefinitely in all directions, binding all
things in a perfect order.

Wisdom in an individual is the capacity to
react to any person or any given situation in
the light of a knowledge of the true nature of
each; it is a principle that embodies itself and
operates in any set of circumstances.

To be conscious of one's ignorance is the beginning of wisdom, and an ignorance of parts will not trouble the man who has achieved a happy sense of relationship with the whole. All truth will come to him who has a living relation to things, since to live is to grow and progress.

Wisdom is not a matter of study, but a matter of living, and of sure action which rises above opposites.

Wisdom cannot be communicated by another, for it is the incommunicable source, which must be discovered by yourself, from which you gather nectar as from an unseen flower.

Wisdom is that nature which blossoms like a rose, when the time comes, in the spiritually barren desert of life in ignorance.

To be wise is to live in an inner harmony that eventually overcomes all outer discords.

We need not head-learning, of which we have plenty, but Soul-Wisdom, the ability to discern the truth behind every mask of self-deception and falsehood. One can carry a vast load of learning, yet be foolish; also, it is possible with a little knowledge to be greatly wise.

To be truly wise is to be truly free. For Wisdom does not lie in prejudice, in a conditioned approach, in seeing things of the present through ideas of the past.

He is the wise man who knows how to use his knowledge, who, while planning to discharge all his responsibilities, lives in a state of essential unconcern as to the future. He is then light-hearted as a bird; without being irresponsible, he can recapture the adventurousness of life.

When Wisdom rules the world, all things in it will be rearranged so as to cause that light which is in each thing and in all men to shine.

Wisdom lies in the search for and discovery of the true ends of life, all of which are comprised in one end, conceive it as perfect happiness, perfect beauty or perfect action.

Wisdom is always the blossoming of the quality of life, revealing life's deep meanings. It is the unity of the all, reflected in the unity of a part. It is a movement of life which shows life in its superlativeness and at its best. It is thought released from every tether, formed by a direct impulse from heaven. It is a divine ray which penetrates both heart and mind and unifies them. It is the breath of God of which the heat is life, and the light is love and beauty.

He is the wise man who has by perfect living gained the instinct of rightness by which he guides himself, whether in thought or action who has found that center of balance which is always over his point of contact with circumstances. He is the man into whom Nature pours the riches of all her instincts.

# V

## LOVE

LOVE is the light of the Soul, in which all
that is perceived is truth—also the fire of the
Spirit by which all that is base is transformed
into good.

Love is a basic state in which there is the
possibility of both understanding and wisdom.

To be one with another is to love him, and
to love him is to act from within him and
through him, and not upon him from without,
with a contrary effect.

Nothing in the world is self-sufficient, except
that which is rooted in a condition of love.

*❧*

The state of love is the state of grace. The
development of that state and the unlocking
of its mysteries brings one to the condition
where there is no separation between oneself
and others.

*❧*

It is in a state of love that all perfections
arise; it is the state in which there is no self-
centeredness.

*❧*

The love which deserves that name is impartial, non-possessive, wholly beneficent; in
that love alone is to be discovered the force
which will ultimately bring man to his freedom.

Love is the only force which does not create
or add to the complications of karma.

Love is the outgoing force of the soul, the
God-in-man.

Love is the solvent of the little self.

Love, devoid of self-gratification, is in essence
the will to the greatest good of another.

Is it not possible for us to be so full of divine
compassion and love that it flows through
every visible and invisible connection we may
have made with our fellow-beings?

Love conquers that separation which is the root-cause of all misunderstanding and trouble; it overleaps the barriers which prevent communion. Increased contact should result in increased affection.

Love is a radiation, an outflow of energy. In pure love toward another there is more than an intensity of benevolence and acceptance of that other, there is a giving forth of what one is, without any straining.

Love is, ideally, the state in which the distinction between self and another has vanished. This does not mean that we abolish individuality, but we learn to regard the happiness, the progress, the interests of another as our own.

Where there is love without possession and
the seeking of any gratification from that
possession, there is bliss.  Thus, to love is to
give oneself without asking for a return, and in
such giving is the experience of joy.

In a state of spiritual or universal Love, all
other persons are but one person—the object
of love.

Love has to become an impersonal flame,
by becoming universal.

No love can be lasting or reach its acme,
which is not touched with some intimation of
the pathos or sublimity of the situation in
which the object of love may be involved.

To love a friend intensely, yet with pure detachment; to let him be equally or even more a friend of others; to expect no affection, while being duly appreciative of whatever affection is given; to think of how one can help, rather than of what gratification one can get; to be constant in friendship and unselfish helpfulness; to bring to the physical level the beautiful, selfless spirit of the higher planes—this is the ideal love.

Ideal love, stepped down to the level of the practical, day-to-day life, must mean the service of each to all within his or her sphere, a delicate consideration of others, a control that gives rise to peace, and cessation from every thought of cruelty and lust.

When love is all in all, it is the Beloved who is present everywhere.

Love must become a creative influence in
our lives, it must be worked into our judgments
and all our plans of action, it should be
translated into service.

Love is the only force known to man which
it is not possible to vanquish by any threat,
however dire, in any ordeal, however terrible,
to which it may be put.   In its purity it inspires
to the most wondrous sacrifice.

As we think thoughts of love down here, all
invisibly we drop seeds in that celestial soil
where they will grow in unimaginable profusion
and beauty.

Without love there is no unfoldment, because love belongs to the life of the Spirit, to the real Self; without love all search is in vain.

Let the one great aim and ideal be to lift up and universalize our affection, so that while it is as deep and intimate as though it has but one object, yet it is ready to be centered on any person, to flow to any point of need.

# VI

## BEAUTY

BEAUTY, not as an abstract principle but in its endless rendering, is the language of God; it translates the infinite, subjective Truth into its appropriate objective expression.

❧

Every beautiful thing is a window through which we can look into the ever-present Reality.

❧

That which is wholly beautiful has an absolutness which is the sign and seal of the hidden Divinity.

❧

A beautiful thing is one in which the consciousness rests content, in which there is neither urge nor need to go beyond and find something else with which to round off and complete the experience.

⚜

To put away the ugly is to follow the subtle clue of Beauty.

⚜

When the manifesting form becomes one of perfect beauty, then the highest significance is released and the life within that form is wholly expressed and fulfilled.

⚜

Nature is evolving beauty, as well as intelligence and capacity. That which is hidden in each thing, the Idea behind it, is in a process of revelation, and will be fully revealed only when the form is perfect and beautiful.

You are infinitely beautiful when you give without one single thought of asking or taking.

Art of every sort, when it embodies Beauty, speaks the language of an invisible order in which each thing has its own significant place.

Beauty is not susceptible to appropriation. If there is any beauty anywhere, it belongs to the very nature of things. It is as erroneous to regard as your possession the beauty of your form as it is to imagine that the beauty of the sunset belongs to yourself or anybody else.

An object of beauty exists for itself, as a revelation of the One Beauty. The highest end that is served, possibly, is that revelation.

I believe in Beauty, abstract and concrete, and in giving oneself to it.

Beauty is the creation of Life, which flows into a form and impresses it with the Truth which is at the very source of that flow.

There is such a thing as a stairway of beauty, a progressive appreciation and sense of the beautiful. Taste has to evolve and reach maturity and refinement.

Beauty in form, Truth in idea, these are the outer and inner correlatives. Each attests the other.

When the idea is beautiful in truth, the expression or the gesture will also be beautiful.

All beauty springs from the same source, and all things beautiful are secretly in affinity with one another.

A beautiful thing is justified in itself, because it is itself, and no other thing.

That which is truly beautiful, whether a work of art or a product of natural evolution, is an intimation from above, from a world of Light, where there is neither the shadow of the past nor of a dubious future created out of an imperfect present.

Beauty at its supreme point, when it is absolute, lifts one out of the object in which it is present. The pure artist works only for the love of his work, with no motive other than his self-abnegating spirit.

The greatest Beauty is beauty of soul, and that beauty has to be realized in thought, in feeling, in behavior, and in every form of action.

We have yet to grow wings for the swan-flight from Time to Eternity, following that archetypal line of Beauty which is but a far-off dream to mortals.

# VII

## UNITY

THE underlying truth of all things, the essential truth of everything that presents itself, is the Unity of Life; the mouldings are different, but the substratum is the same.

Unity is an overmastering principle which gradually masters each diversity and brings it within the scope of an integrated expression.

The deeper we plumb the philosophic basis of our thought with regard to the nature of existence, the more do we realize the necessity for a principle of Unity in the universe, if the universe is capable of a philosophic summing-up.

Whatever the gradations by which the One becomes the many, by those same gradations the many have to re-become the One.

All the children of God—men, animals, trees, minerals, elemental lives—shall together go back to their common Parent, but in union amongst themselves.

Under the influence of his own higher mind, which is even now appearing above the horizon, man must synthesize and prove by action that difference need not clash with difference, but should be built up into a unity.

Unity is the deepest underlying fact of all. When from that Unity there goes forth the

Word or impulse which is bodied in the manifested universe, it seems as if the Unity is lost,
but in reality it is only hidden.

Whether in a speck of dust, or in a leaf or
flower, or in the least living thing, it is the One
Life which exists as the innermost reality, the
Truth of truths.

Unity is an immaculate wholeness.

From the One Reality, which is neither Spirit
nor Matter but both, life issues, and issuing
flows endlessly in streams, branching more and
more into innumerable single lives, each specialized in its way, thus manifesting an infinite
diversity of effects, qualities and capabilities.
This process reaching its limit, the differentiated

lives turn back to unite, thus to rebecome the Unity they ever were.

In Unity there is no self and no otherness. There is only the One who reveals Himself in incomparable modes.

The light of Unity breaking through the screen of separation constitutes the glory of life.

The truth which is in ourselves, but lost by our minds, is the truth of Unity, which is behind everything and related to everything.

The sense of Unity is the core of true service.

Separateness must break itself, and unity prevail.

The temple of humanity will not have its walls complete except by the increasing sharing by all men of the world's varied treasures of thought and beauty.

Inwardly let me relate myself to all, and offer that relationship to the One who blesses all union.

Without the principle of Unity there can be no coherence, no hope and no certainty of harmony in a world of turmoil and diversity.

Man needs to realize the unity of mankind,
which means brotherhood translated into justice
in his dealings, harmony in his thoughts and
feelings, and cooperation in action.

We transcend the little self and develop the
awareness of our unity with others only as we
go out in love which seeks to help and serve.

Since humanity is one, in some manner our
own thoughts, prayers, aspirations and efforts
must tell in the shaping of all men's thoughts and
actions.

Man is an individual, but also part of a
living whole, a throbbing, radiating being,
whose influences for good and ill must be poured
into the lives of others, and theirs received into

his.   He cannot evolve except in relation to his fellow-beings.

The practice of the unity amidst the differences makes a man spiritual in his life as he is spiritual in essence, and will prepare him for the knowledge of the Truth, which is the Divine Wisdom.

There is a design for all humanity, which will be manifested only as humanity becomes a whole, a design which will make clear all that has gone before.

Proclaim it in any way we may, in any beautiful form, with any illustrations, if we can produce the consciousness of a Unity in all the diversity, a kinship between all animated forms, we will be bestowing on the world the greatest blessing.

# VIII

## INDIVIDUALITY

In each man, however humble, there is the hidden gem of his own individuality, and we must admit the worth of each gem and its right to a setting where it can shine with such lustre as it commands.

❧

That which is free of all conditioning, untouched by any extraneous influence, is individual; it is distinguished.

❧

Each individual thing stands apart from the rest of the universe and all other things therein. In this standing apart lies its self-definition.

It is the aloneness of its individuality which gives it its rightful significance.

If you regard all forms in Nature as constituting a Universal Form, and the quality, the nature, the individuality of each form as the note it strikes, the whole evolutionary process is a movement toward a state in which the individuality of each separate thing is brought to its finest point, and all individualities are synthesized in one universal order which makes a supreme and all-comprehending Individual.

Individuality has a meaning, a significance, a certain law within it, which makes it what it is, and nothing else.

We stand out in our individual uniqueness as we reach our perfection, and that uniqueness is not something made but something natural, self-born and self-existent.

The higher the degree of individuality in any thing, the more self-contained it is, the more austere, the more its dignity and integrity.

When man is taken up into Godhead, he does not lose his unique quality, but as an individual he is taken into a comprehensive pattern which gives a new meaning to every separate part.

Each specialized part, every fragment of Life, has its uniqueness, its exclusive value, its special note.

When we are vital yet detached, uninfluenced
by the thoughts of others except to consider
them carefully, then we may discover as in an
inner sanctum the secret of our own self, the
way we have to tread to our appointed goal.

The true character of an individual should
be apparent to others and not to himself; it is
only as we forget ourselves that we shine forth
with our true beauty.

In the unfoldment of his living, each man's
self becomes a law, a rhythm and an individuality
—individuality not in the sense of a consciousness that feels separate, but illustrating his
own eternal, individual characteristics.

When an individuality is perfectly expressed
in a form, the essence of that individuality is

a certain unity in that form, an order of its
parts, which perfectly integrates those parts.

Each individual has in him something unique,
a law of is own being, worked out in terms of
his evolution.

It is only when the form fits the inner Spirit
and is exuberant with Life, and every human
cell tingles with the vitality of its own creative
power, that the individuality stands out with
its proper dignity and majesty.

## IX

## FREEDOM

FREEDOM is obedience to universal Law, and we feel most free when we obey the law of our own being.  That law is within us, and seeks expression through us.

The Ancient Wisdom proclaims to man the precious nature of his freedom, and shows that by appealing to his noblest instincts we can build an order combining freedom with security, stability with progress, and creativity with cooperation.

Freedom belongs to the Spirit, determinism to matter.

The first and most important step to freedom from the conditioning by our past is to feel its desirability.  When we see the goal in the clearest light of objectivity, the goal is here and now, present amidst the conditioning.

True freedom consists in understanding ourselves, our thoughts, our motives, our wants and behavior.

When the nature of the Spirit, which is free everywhere and always, prevails, there is freedom for each and all; each is then a center of peace and harmony, also a center for the creation of those values which are inherent in the Spirit.

Freedom is the mother of originality, for true creation is born of freedom, unmixed with anything extraneous to itself.

There is experience of freedom when there is no inhibition or urge from self, no inner discord, but only a satisfying sense of order and harmony.

He enjoys no freedom who has no control over himself. Man needs the order of an inner harmony, which implies mastery over himself.

Freedom is self-determination, not a reaction compelled or mechanical. He who is a slave to his passions, who is driven by habits of thought, emotion or action set up or contracted in ignorance, is not a free man.

Freedom is the fundamental requisite for happiness; without freedom life has no room in which to expand, it is choked and stifled.

Freedom cannot be separated from order, which implies control, whether in society or in oneself.

To be free is to be happy without seeking happiness, to act with a spontaneous motion which is the resultant of an inward grace.

Action according to the law of your own being is true freedom.

When there is any motion—of thought, feeling, or action—which is generated in freedom, and not as a reaction compelled from without by something external to that motion, the result is spontaneity, delight and originality.

Freedom is first of all a freedom from oneself as a product of the past, because the influence of the past is a limitation of the present.

True freedom is an inward state; it is freedom from passion and fear, from craving for support, from every kind of influence which is a detraction from the clear vision of truth.

When freedom is an inner compulsion, free will and necessity are compounded and reconciled.

We are most free when we are free from ourselves. Our fullest freedom lies in perfect service.

Freedom, even as a common experience, lies in being able to be oneself. It consists in acting from a point which is compelled neither from without nor from within.

When the consciousness is free of craving for sensation, free of the conditions which it has undergone, free of the compulsion to plan and build for any self-gratifying end, then it can follow every wandering breeze, mould itself to the inner being of every significant form, and yet not be moulded.

We are free only when we serve the One Supreme Being, the ever-free unconditioned Self.

The four freedoms of the aspirant: To desist from possessions and security; the abolition of fear; the discovery of one's own way; and instinctive individual action.

※

Without love of freedom and faith in freedom, there is no hope of creating a world of freedom and preserving it.

※

Let us aim at creating freedom and happiness for others rather than for ourselves. Then will success be more likely than if we acted with a self-centered aim.

※

When we give up, from the inmost self of ourselves, everything to which the mind of sense and desire is attached, there is freedom within. In that freedom our soul-star shines and spreads its light through every one of its vestures.

※

# X

## REALITY

THE Reality which, according to those who can speak of it, is indescribable, one and complete and unchanging, cannot be unrelated to the changes in the realm of diversity. The worlds of form and consciousness are but a mirror for its reflections.

The highest Reality must be in those forms of harmony which are possible to the purest comprehension.

The Reality is within ourselves, but it requires a consciousness purified of the dross of desire and indulgences to feel it and to know it.

Life is real, and Reality lies in its fullness, as experienced in any state of consciousness whose depth and extension are undisturbed by whatever occupies or fills that state.

The Real is made manifest in consciousness by identity between the Real and the consciousness. It needs a consciousness which is not already occupied but is a free and open ground into which it can move.

The Reality that is sought by us must be an unknown; whereas all concepts based on experience are memories of the known. They belong to a past which overshadows the present.

The only Reality must be in the unity pervading all diversities.

We have to learn to interpret the truths of physical nature in a manner which constitutes them a mirror for viewing the many-aspected mystery of the Spirit.

The Real, in its widest sense, must include a comprehension beyond our present senses, including shades of feelings not in our present range, as well as forms built out of the material of those feelings.

The Reality, though one, manifests in gradations, at each level as a whole sufficient unto itself and unto him who experiences it. It is a whole in significance and not merely a relationship of parts.

Reality shines all the time like the sun, but it can dawn upon us only when we are ready for it, when we turn ourselves round to receive its light.

The man who has found Reality can have no other aim or desire than the supreme good and happiness of all beings, of all life in every form.  He is increasingly one with them, and they are one in him.

# XI

## HARMONY

WHEREVER Life is, there is the process of building; different elements are brought together into relations which make of them a living whole, capable of functioning together in harmony.

The endeavor of Nature through man, and of man as he learns his identity with her, is to create an order of harmony and beauty out of the material that comes into human life and is meant for human use.

Harmony is unity in diversity.

Harmony dwells in self-control. It brings the two poles of existence into union with each other. It turns all opposites into complementaries. It is the means of giving oneself to those around oneself. It constitutes the essence of yoga, and makes one's whole being a perfect channel through which all that one is in Eternity may flow forth into one's time-manifestation.

A rhythmic harmony in oneself and an outward-turned sensitiveness is the foundation for yoga, in which there is union between knower and known in a state of harmony comprehending both.

When we have succeeded in harmonizing ourselves, it is not a static condition that we achieve, but a growing harmony, in which any new note that is introduced does not mar the whole composition, but has the effect of elaborating and enriching it.

We must be in a state of perfect harmony and mutual friendliness in order to bring down into manifestation the forces which would otherwise remain and operate at levels beyond our reach.

The most perfect harmony is really an absolute unity, where the action of every part is so joined with that of every other that the total effect is simple and unique, like a perfect chord.

We have to become translucent, instead of opaque as we mostly are, and bring about that harmony between the inner and the outer, the higher and the lower, which is a condition of true understanding and fitness.

Our energies have become involved in a matrix of inharmonies; they have to be evolved into the harmony of an eternal order.

Perfect harmony is perfect balance, and the true aspirant is he who balances the necessary qualities in himself, in whom there is not the unbalance of an exaggeration nor faltering from an essential principle.

In the Self there is unity, an involved or subjective harmony without which there would be no integration, nor the bliss that must co-exist with that harmony.

What we need to achieve is the unification of our nature, the harmonization of its different parts, so that they may constitute a coherent and abiding whole.

Each one is a theme in the Divine Harmony, though we are in different stages of unfoldment of that theme.

That end which is the perfection to which all Nature, including man, is moved by the very impulsion of the forces hidden within her, must be a universal harmony in which each life, clothed in its appropriate form, finds its most effective and fitting place.

## XII

## HAPPINESS

ONLY when we live with abandonment of self, with absolute self-surrender, with no element of inhibition, no urge, no obstruction, shall we know what freedom means, and thus experience the truest happiness.

Happiness is a timeless and undivided state which belongs not to the part, but to the whole.

Happiness is a fulfilment which cannot be sought as a selfish goal, but comes with the forgetting of self.

It is in the casting off of every psychological fetter, in the dissolution of every suppressed complex that freedom lies, and in it is the highest joy.

In a happy state there is no wanting of more; there is an expansion to capacity, a tension which neither falls short nor is over-exerted.

Be a factor in the happiness of others. The only true happiness is that which never remains with oneself, but, as it is experienced, is passed on to others.

There is a pure happiness that arises out of virtue, right living, life without fears, without

wants, and without possession, but only with
a divine simplicity.

Happiness is a pure and simple cup that is
devoid both of excitation and opiates, of the
poison of an ever-recurring thirst, as well as
the oblivion of indifference to others, a cup
that ever measures full.

There is a serene happiness that springs
from gravity, composure and a sense of the
dignity and power innate in life.

Expected happiness is based on recollections
of the past, which are as a cloud upon the
present.  It is the unexpected joy which is the
highest joy.

Each must discover in himself that which is capable of a beautiful expansion, which will be a protection and blessing to others, the means of releasing the light in himself. In that light and that expansion is the joy of Divinity.

# XIII

## PEACE

THE sense of peace arises from harmony with the essential nature of things, an inwardly undistorted and beautiful relationship to everybody and everything.

The world needs peace, and the prime requisite for peace is goodwill between members of different races and nations, between adherents of different faiths and cultures.

There can be no peace to him who carries a sword in his heart, because even as it turns in his dreams it will hurt the man who harbors it.

Peace is the happy, natural state of man and of all Nature's children.

Peace arises from a state of inward freedom from disordering effects and from distorting pressures; it is also a state of fundamental reconciliation between one person and another.

The lower self can find peace only as it merges into and becomes a reflection of the higher.

Peace is not the absence of fighting on some front, an uneasy lull, but an integrated condition which arises from a perfect harmonization of all the processes of life.

It is impossible to feel peace unless one has positive goodwill towards others, not just to one's special friends and allies, and denied to others.

❧

Right thought, right feeling, right action—these are the way to peace.

❧

In the world at large there can be no peace of a lasting order, none worth speaking of, or deserving that name, without peace in ourselves.

❧

Peace is bound up with righteousness. Until there is justice, right dealing, until the relations between peoples are governed by the Law of Brotherhood, true peace will be a chimera.

❧

In the heart of a world, composed as Nature has composed it, peaceful, integrated and progressive, man must take his place as a peace-loving entity, ever open to fresh life and ideas.

※

A total organization of human life for a total peace is the vessel needed to launch humanity on a happy new era.

※

If so much can be done for war, cannot the same be attempted for peace—a beautiful, constructive, secure peace, enfolding all differences of faith, race, culture, nationality and thought, and stimulating each to flame into its individual brilliance?

※

Peace is not a matter of rules, a disposition of forces, an adjustment, or a problem in mechanics. It is created by goodwill in the hearts of people, whence it is diffused through their lives.

The dove of peace has first to find a resting-place for its feet in our hearts, before it can make its home in our surroundings, establish itself in the environment of our being.

If we are peace-minded, we enjoy peace within, even when there is conflict and violence without.

Peace is not a matter for bargaining. It has to be established in oneself by realizing its rightness, and then expressed in all modes of thought and action, in dealing with one's fellows and with the lesser kingdoms of Nature as well.

There will be peace within ourselves and throughout the world only when there is respect for the universal law and order, for that law which is Nature's law and the Divine dispensation which we can observe in the universal process. Only when we accept and submit absolutely to that dispensation can there be peace in our own hearts and in our world.

## XIV

## HELPFULNESS AND SERVICE

WHAT is it to help? Not dictation nor inter-
ference nor making the other person an image
of ourselves, but to give of ourselves un-
reservedly in that modulated form which will
blend with the life in the person whom we
seek to help.

There can be no greater purpose in life than
to serve—service to the One in many forms.
It must not be so-called, limited service but
real service, which is direct and sincere, which
has in it that spirit of self-sacrifice which we
would display in a crisis.

The way of unity is love manifested as service.

It is only when there is realization of our unity with our fellow-beings, and when the only motive is that of giving ourselves in such service as we are capable, that we can fill our lives with rich, helpful and creative action.

In the truest service the consciousness of self is forgotten—you help because you cannot do other than help.

We must learn to serve with all our faculties, with all the means at our disposal, each expressing the individuality of his own place in the scheme of things by adapting himself, as he stands, to the needs of each and every situation.

To open one's heart, to become resistance-less and barrier-less, is the means of true understanding, as well as of pouring out any possible help. Let the kingdom of your heart be so wide that no one is excluded.

Regard every contact as an opportunity to help, yet know also that it is a means for self-purification.

Given an attitude of openness, we can help others and ourselves. Without understanding, our best efforts to help will only hinder. Under-standing cannot be achieved except with a sympathetic reception of the other man's feelings, from which arise his point of view.

We have to learn to give ourselves in service, in all places and in all manner needed and possible.

" How can I help you?" must be the constant query in relation to one and all.

✌

Only as we go out in love, which seeks to help and serve, do we transcend ourselves and develop that consciousness which embodies the awareness of our essential unity with others.

✌

The work of helping others—humanity and the individuals about us—must become all-absorbing.

✌

Make of life a perfect form for the expression of the spirit of helpfulness and its play upon the world.

✌

To help but to be unconscious of helping, not to know that one is blessing, but to convey the fullness of every possible blessing—is

that not the marvel which takes place when a
person is truly and altogether kind and helpful?

If you would be of real service, you must
be full of reverence for the inner self which is
seeking to express itself in its own way in every
other individual. You must approach the
person to be helped in an attitude of seeking
to understand, in an attitude of respect. Then
if you can give him something which will be
of value on his particular path and at the
particular stage of his treading it, that is true
service.

Instead of being bound by the narrow circle
of our separate interests and attachments, we
have to live from a center of radiating forces
which do not return to us—live in an attitude
of giving and helping.

There is a holiness in pure, unexpectant service.

When we think of helping the world, of being brothers to all, we should remember that the world means also the unwanted who knock at our door at an inopportune moment, the people whom we may dislike for some reason, physical or mental, those whose appearance or ways may be disagreeable to our tastes, and those whom we might be ashamed of, if we were of that company.

One has to forge oneself into an instrument of service. This involves a radical reorganization of the whole nature, a work which lies less on the outer plane than on the planes of one's inner being. This reorganization amounts to a spiritual rebirth, and Brotherhood is its basis.

To proclaim the truths of the higher life and live them is the service required of all of us.

Man's true greatness lies in being nothing, in abolishing himself, while his good works spread on every side.

When all life becomes a poem of service, in the true, pure, inward sense, then all life grows exceedingly beautiful; it unfolds like a flower.

Awaken in each one whom you contact the best impulses, the purest and the most beautiful in him; enrich and sweeten the surrounding atmosphere with thoughts of blossoming God-head; this is indeed service, most beautiful and lasting.

## XV

## HUMILITY AND SIMPLICITY

SIMPLICITY lies in a direct and uncomplicated approach both to persons and things, so that we see them and meet them as they are. It is only a simple mind which can understand and resolve complexities.

Simplicity is a clean separation of essentials from non-essentials, of the true from the false, and a perfect integration of thought and feeling.

That which is simple is susceptible to no action from outside. He who is simple at heart is not affected by injuries.

Humility is not mere consciousness of our littlenesses, which might be only a feeling of disappointment at not being as important as we would wish to be, nor is it self-depreciation. Rather is it the eradication of all self-conceit, so that we become sweet and beautiful, have an openness of mind and heart, and feel a really deep respect for another, whoever he may be, based on the recognition of his Godhead.

To be simple in one's aims is to be one-pointed, a natural streamlining which adapts the means to the end, thus to move forward with economy of effort.

We must be busy trying to know ourselves, which is to detach ourselves and simplify ourselves.

The simplicity which reduces everything to its essential values is the mark of the spiritual man. It is discrimination between the essential and the non-essential.

It is a mistake to think that service of a humble character is not of importance. It is the attitude of the server which is most important.

Simplicity has meaning because it says a little and conveys a great deal; it is defined by what it rejects as well as by what it includes.

Simplicity is a divine quality which in a work of art is an expression of its unity; in Life, of its one-pointedness.

Be simple—not with the simplicity of negation, but with the profundity of comprehension.

Humility bespeaks the proximity of greatness, the near event of the emptying of the waters of oneself into the ocean to which they belong.

Be simple to the last degree, therefore infinitely capable.

True simplicity springs not from ignorance, but from maturity of wisdom.

True humility becomes the source of our wisdom; the more a man knows, the more he realizes how little he knows, and the most wise is the most humble.

Humility is a condition of uttermost self-forgetfulness, an intensely sensitive spiritual state.

Simplicity is an art which is divine, and it is artless.  It is the emergence of the unity from diversity.

True simplicity lies in a relation of direct-ness.  When you see things as they are, you are simple, and you have resolved all complexes.

When all things naturally and spontaneously serve one single purpose, there is simplicity; for life is simple at the center, where unity prevails.

The deeper the source of one's action, the simpler and truer it is, potent in its purity and resolving in its effects.

Only in that simplicity which is a perfect emptiness, as well as an undivided wholeness, is it possible to discover the beauty that is everywhere, the beauty which is capable of being expressed in one's own life or to be perceived in another.

## XVI

## SYMPATHY AND KINDNESS

SYMPATHY is a state in oneself which responds to the quality of each living thing in nature. It has as many shades as there are forms to utter life's endlessly varied meanings.

Sympathy is essentially sensitiveness, a feeling with, responding to, without any kind of resistance.

Kindliness is a true touchstone; it magnetizes a man for all pure influences.

Sympathy makes for the most intimate understanding; it adjusts perfectly to everyone and everything; it is the parent of softness and of healing.

Sympathy, appreciation, every beautiful response to things, all that enables one to take the other person to one's heart—these are the modes by which one comes into direct contact with, and, hence, understanding of another.

You can sympathize with the most vicious person if you will go behind the hardened external crust.

We have to create for ourselves a body of compassion in which our fellow-beings will be cells.

Cultivate a dynamic gentleness which makes others gentle.

The man of perfect sympathy can draw from the infinite storehouse of thought and feeling those forces and qualities which best suit his purposes.

Every form of understanding springing out of a sympathetic relationship is a means of increasing harmony.

The less we use the world for our own purposes and depend upon it as a parasite, the more we shall be able to sympathize with those who are in it, and help them in their struggles.

We help others, not by interfering with their lives nor by imposing our ideas on them, but always by acting in a spirit of sympathy and self-identification with them in their troubles and joys.

Let the basis for our help be kindliness and an all-round sympathy which produces balance. That balance, which is the correction of every element of one-sidedness, comes out of appreciating the quality of each thing and person as it is and as he or she is, without comparisons and judgments.

A kind thought has more value than a material gift, because it cannot be bought.

Forget yourself, and think of the stars, the boundless expanse of the sky, the fair flowers in the field, the wonderful truths you can comprehend, the sympathy, the encouragement you can give to someone in need, in short, almost anything except yourself and your wants.

## XVII

## GIVING AND RECEIVING

THERE is an infinity in each one of us to give; we have to discover the mode of giving it.

We have to learn to give with our hearts. When we help from the very soul of ourselves, there can be no consciousness of a helper separate from the one who is being helped.

The law of life on the upward path is the law of giving or sacrifice, which is not privation but the purest joy for the mind and heart irradiated by a divine impulse.

Never fail in pouring out love, in spite of any real or imagined lack of response.

So long as we are poised in the dilemma, to give or not to give, we have not yet come to that point where it is possible to give completely, purely, naturally and joyfully.

A man who wants nothing can give all.

Giving is the true nature of ourselves. In what to give and how to give it lies the art of spiritual living.

To give without reserve and constantly of the best that one has and is, to each within one's circle of contact and action, must be the law of one's life.

Sacrifice is not pain nor privation, but fulfillment.

It is possible to give oneself, to abandon oneself to all that is divine, sacred and beautiful everywhere and in everything.

With each there is a perfect adjustment possible. By such adjustment one both gives and receives.

To hold everything that one possesses—worldly goods, talents, time, energy—as a trustee for the welfare of each and all is the mark of the illuminated man.

Let it be the best in you which you give to others. Our graciousness has most value where there is most need.

We have to set up in ourselves that outward-turned motion which is the spirit of giving. The nature of matter is to acquire, possess and fortify itself; the nature of the Spirit is to hold nothing, to give of itself and all that it controls, according to its wisdom.

You must give your heart to each and all of the many, before it can center itself in the One.

Give and be satisfied in the giving, for as has been truly stated, love is its own eternity.

It is only when we are giving, rather than taking, that we are able to purify all the channels of our nature and enable the forces of love to well up and overflow in every direction.

When you give your interest, your goodwill, your sympathy, your understanding, you make a pure relationship. Let there be nothing more to it than just that giving.

⚘

If the attitude is wholly one of giving, all problems are bound to cease. In such an attitude is true dignity.

⚘

Let me give myself in constant and unreserved love to all beings whom I have ever known, and seek in my heart their perpetual good.

⚘

When giving has become the law of self expression, Life pours all her riches into you.

⚘

To give in flawless selflessness, to give ever more and more, becomes the end and aim in life for the aspirant.

Those enduring values which are in ourselves can neither be kept to ourselves nor diminished by being given to others.

## XVIII

## BROTHERHOOD

Brotherhood is the only right relationship, because we are sharers of one and the same Life.

Remember that each individual is a letter in the alphabet of God; each, whether past, present or future, a theme in the Divine Harmony; each a grain of sand on the shore of Eternity.

The brotherly attitude means taking each person as he is, regarding him with affection, and helping him in the most natural manner and with the grace that is born of not expecting any return. None of us really knows the potentialities of another, what are his true qualities and capacities, to what heights he will presently rise.

He who gives himself to the cause of brotherhood will find endless strength and inspiration for himself.

We have descended into differentiation of every type; we must ascend into the unity of our brotherhood.

Brotherhood, the one truth of practical action and ethics, is a dynamic impulse, which each will translate in his own way and according to his means and conditions.

The more different I am from others, the more I need to be supplemented by them in the Work.

Brotherhood is a comprehending arc, recognizing the differences but not forgetting the unity; it is a pure relation, without possession, friendly and free.

The world has to be totally and effectively organized for peace, freedom and co-operation, which are the practical manifestations of brotherhood.

Dedicate yourself to each one of your fellow-beings.

To him who seeks the Truth, brotherhood is a touch-stone; it must take precedence of every doctrine.

❧

We must understand a brother as he is. Since each one is, in himself, beyond the bounds of any definition, any statement of the truth about another can be only a partial statement.

❧

What the world needs most of all is brotherhood, first in the heart of man, and next, as its reflection in the outer world, an integration of its scattered parts and functions.

❧

The brotherhood of races, of nations, of classes, of sexes and ages must be our constant aim, keeping the distinctions where they are natural, but harmonizing them for their total and individual enrichment.

Brotherhood must become not just an objective rule but, equally, an ever-present reality, with ever more and more men and women burning with zeal to carry it out in practice.

Let us accept no creed, no practice, no institution which does not answer the test of brotherhood.

# XIX

## SPIRITUALITY

SPIRITUALITY is a quality of the inmost being, which permeates the whole realm of one's consciousness, and causes an outflow of mind and heart from the purest sources of oneself.

The spiritual state is a state of grace that comes by itself as we cease from the error of our ways, in our thought, motives and action. The spirit moves into whatever form is adapted to receive it.

Spirituality is the golden mean of self-abnegation.

The spiritual man is one who has broken through all illusion and pretence, and has unified himself. His dreams are dreams at one end and creations at the other.

❧

The spiritual state is not a condition which is set or static, not a placid immobility, but a state of dynamism and balance. It is both negative and positive; negative for understanding, positive for action.

❧

Spiritual living is a fulfilment from moment to moment, in which the outer person is in a state of living rapport with the inner being and becomes an extension thereof.

❧

The spiritual man has few wants, for he does not dwell upon the pleasures of the past, nor does he cling to the satisfactions of the present.

In the realm of the Spirit, to know is to love; its knowledge is knowledge of the essence of things.

Being spiritual does not consist in leaving the world, putting on a special garb, performing particular ceremonies, being religious in any conventional sense. The spiritual state is a state of consciousness and being, it is an integration of mind and spirit.

The man who aims at perfect spiritual fitness in his living has to transcend all craving of whatever sort, every weakness which asks for indulgence, and attain a state of complete self-mastery, as well as absolute non-possession.

Spirituality is not dull respectability nor pious conformity, but a life exquisite, intense, full of romance, alluring and mysterious.

The spiritual Self is the hidden God in man, the touch-stone of reality to all that he is and does, whose every creation is a manifestation of harmony, a revelation of truth.

The Spirit has no race, no nationality, no religion. It is outside all identifications. He who is spiritual feels free to look at things from *any* point of view, and is committed to nothing partial or exclusive.

The spiritual man is one who has transcended the play of opposites and has integrated himself. Because of his wholeness he can meet each one with the whole of his being. Each thing he takes into his consciousness becomes, in its inner nature, one with himself.

Spiritual living is living in the most natural manner, without pretence or pose, lightly and easily, in accordance with the nature of the Spirit, so that all thought, all feeling and all action partake of that nature and flow in the direction determined by the Spirit itself.

The spiritual man is one whose heart is empty of all personal aims and desires, and open to all beings everywhere, therefore one with all beings and things.

Spiritual living is a life of action all the time, but action which arises from no self-regarding motive. It is action in the true sense, and not reaction.

The spiritual man is like a child in his inno-
cence, naturalness and simplicity, though he
be the well of Wisdom itself.

He who desires to follow the way of purity,
which is spirituality, has to move away from
the world, its modes of thought, and the reactions current and fashionable among those
who make the world what it is.

Spiritual living is creative living, to which all
that is inharmonious or productive of misery
is a challenge.

The change which spirituality implies is a
perfect harmonization, the creation of a unity
out of the diverse possibilities in ourselves,

until every movement that takes place within, along with the action that follows without, becomes part of a symphony that expresses in time what one is in eternity.

He who wants to live spiritually is not concerned with power or position, with prestige, flattery, importance or domination, all of which have to disappear if he is to tread the way of his own inner rightness.

The spiritual man accepts all that comes to him and, seeking nothing, is in harmony with all.

When you feel near to your fellowmen, you are near to the path of holiness or spirituality.

If each of us can be a spiritual lotus, we will be able to fill the world with the pure fragrance of the Spirit, and diffuse in the minds and hearts of men a happiness and a hope not there at present.

## XX

## THE ART OF LIVING

THE art of living—the very word "art" implies instinctual action, not action determined by a set of rules or code, though such action may obey certain laws. The art lies in an exploration of harmony, in following the guidance of an unerring pulse, in improving a niceness of adjustment.

The strings of our daily life are few in number, but we can make endless melody thereon.

The only law of living is the law that heips others; to the extent that you forget yourself, you are free to help the world.

Be always tranquil and dignified, gracious and smiling, remembering the Lord of Kailāsa, that peak of loneliness and absolute detachment which yet sends forth an intense radiation of benignance.

There is a way of living so vitally, freshly, originally, spontaneously and dynamically that life becomes a transformation, a state of perpetual joy, a native ecstasy which nothing can take away.

The art of happy, of beautiful living, is living according to Nature's laws, in harmony with that subtle universal order into which all things must inevitably ascend. When a man is in that state of harmony, he is at peace with himself and with others; he becomes a channel for those forces which will create peace and happiness for all.

Be human in the fullest, most beautiful sense, shedding gentle consideration, delicacy and graciousness, but with an exquisite detachment.

You cannot move without leaving footprints, which some may follow.

It is for us to discover that point which is the goal, the summation of our aspirations, as well as the origin of our present being, and when we have discovered that point, that will be a theme which is all-sufficing, which all life can develop into an ever-enlarging symphony, knit together by an infallible logic.

Live beautifully, with infinite graciousness, abandoning all self-seeking, pure as the lotus which is unconscious of itself.

Our sole concern should be the duty of the moment, the duty that comes from the recognizable past, and the duty, which is a joy, of living as helpfully, as beautifully as we can from moment to moment.

To live is not merely to experience, but also to act. There can be no right action without understanding. The essence of all understanding lies in experiencing the very being of the object to be understood.

Train yourself to live in a situation for a time, without even seeking to resolve it.

To live naturally is really to live in inward freedom of heart and mind. Natural, in this sense, means according to and in harmony with one's original, ever uncorrupt, undistorted nature.

The art of living lies not in living alone, but also in living and working with others, understanding them and co-operating for any good purpose held in common.

To live in constant communion with all of life, to learn to make the supreme sacrifice with the will at all times, to know how to give, to make the gift divine, what can be more beautiful than this?

Live in the eternal now, like a bird which has no concern for the morrow. Release yourself from fears born of unhappy memories,

equally from pre-conceived hopes of fulfillment, from all that is a product of the mechanical
aspects of the mind.

To live creatively is not merely to create
something out of an occasional stirring in
oneself, but to recreate or regenerate ourselves
so that we may be able to create out of an
unfailing current in ourselves.

Live every moment as though you were
building a perfect temple.

Exquisiteness is a quality to be aimed at in
language, taste and manners.

We can act in the least little thing with the significance, precision and artistry of the vast cosmic plan. Each incident, each situation, can be made a perfect picture, and it must be made significant by our participation in it.

The fine art of living consists in each one determining for himself his own standards, and not living as a mere reflection of the crowd.

All our actions must bear the true signature of our purpose; our entire being, collected and balanced, should be brought to bear upon each point of action, so that, however little or simple that action, it has within itself an infinity of meaning.

Make every greeting a perfect greeting; every daily act a divine gesture.

Let every moment be perfect in itself and a beautiful prelude to the next, not by anticipating what is to come in vain expectation and hope, but by completeness in meeting the demands of the present.

Live with the mind and the emotions in their most comprehensive sweep, yet with a delicate and discriminating touch; fix every situation on its most significant and limitless background; know by self-identification every nuance of thought and feeling of others within your range; maintain just that tone and tension which every wandering breeze can throw into a melody.

The pearl of great price is in yourself, but you have to find it in a perfection realized in your life.

The world may be dull; if so, you must brighten it by your presence.

There is an art of living, which is greater than any other art. When that art is mastered, then and then only is the person truly accomplished, marked by an all-round development.

If our lives are stagnant, it is because there is no flow of interest to others, no communion with the life around us, our relations with others are partial and largely without life.

Life is for the living. Only those live truly who, even though it may be in little acts, snatches and phrases, give utterance to that endless music, goodness and beauty which is within oneself in store and in possibility.

We must be perfectionists in every particular. Our character is built in our everyday lives, moulded by our reactions to every little circumstance. The universe is so built as to bring out the best in each one of us, little as we may realize it.

We have to mould each part of our living, our every thought and action, nearer to the goal of our aspiration.

Speak each word, perform each action, face each situation before an inner altar where you kneel in uttermost adoration and self-surrender, under the seal and sign of your highest Self.

# XXI

## TOWARD THE STARS

THERE is a Star of Eternity, to which we are guided by the revolutions of Time.

There is a star that presides over our birthing and setting, a star that revolves eternally with ourselves; it is the star of our destiny.

The light of the distant star can come close to the heart of him who is open to its rays.  It is the star of his own being, which constitutes that being.

The perfect form or chalice, which is our eternal individuality, is hid from our imperfect sight by a veil of time woven on the golden loom of God.

Each one of us is, in truth, a spiritual orb of light and beauty waiting to be realized.

There is always the bright and morning star which glitters above the horizon of our ignorance.

Within your own heart is the boundless expanse of cognition. Therein can be viewed every one of those realities which are the stars illuminating your sky.

What is important is the direction we take, our orientation. We cannot know the magnitude of the Star, but can find its true direction as we progress, which progress is in reality a knowledge of what it is, in relation to what we are deep within ourselves.

Our life revolves round a distant pole, the far-off end. That pole remains fixed among the stars of our heaven.

The time comes when the Life-Star culminates in the heavens, and no longer has to come out thereafter. There is no more setting, therefore no more rising; it remains perpetually in the heavens.

The perfection, the potentiality of the loveliness which is in everything, is inevitable. It is the eternal Star which over-masteringly brings all processes to their appointed end, and presides over our voyage through life.

We are as caged eagles; but even from behind the bars we may have a look at the expansive heavens, and draw inspiration from a star.

Man is in his inner being a tiny star which rises and sets many times on earthly life, but eventually, its brightness raised to a superior power, free from attachment to a restricted personality, it takes its place in the heavens. Such stars constitute the glory of our spiritual sky.

The seed of our perfection is the Monad, the parent-principle of our nature, the lone Star whose glimmering ray illumines the otherwise dark chamber of our consciousness.

Our inner state has to be so established that it is ever open towards a mid-heaven, or revolves round a pole-star which will crown with its beneficent rays every aspect of our life.

Each individual is as a star in a host of stars with which the celestial sphere is ablaze, all revolving round that pole-star which is the Star of all existence.

The higher the source of your illumination, the smaller the shadow you cast. Dwell in the shadowless light.

Let us be ever faithful to the Star within us, which is at the same time mysteriously the Master as well as our highest, purest, most unconditioned Self wherein unity and peace abide.

# XXII

## THE MASTER

THE Adepts of our system are its fruit and blossom; and the coming forth of each of them means a new richness in humanity's blood, a new power for its accelerated expressions. They are the evolved modes of consciousness which in the appointed order take precedence of the rest, and become the awakened medium for the redemption of the world from its original deadness, incoherence and ignorance. From the point of view of the downward-looking Spirit, they offer themselves as the Sacrifice that forms the cross of the Spirit upon the bosom of matter, so far as our scheme of evolution is concerned.

Each Great One, as he is called upon to play his part in the scheme, impresses upon his work the mark of his own individuality. We must copy their example.

The Master is more than an objective Man; he is a subjective entity, a reality which is felt only in the heart.

Each life is an impulse from the Divine. In the Master the impulse has burgeoned forth and revealed the fullness of its innate beauty.

In the nature of the Perfect Man, it is the Spirit which predominates, not matter.

It is only when there is perfect mastery over ourselves, and our whole nature can be gathered up into a unity, that we can offer ourselves entirely to the Master and the offer can be real.

The Master is, above all, an embodiment of Truth, and to follow the Master is to follow that Truth which is equally in ourselves.

The Adepts are the efflorescence of the age. In their presence one feels as in a veritable garden of flowers.

As there dawns upon us in our appreciation of things the hitherto unrevealed majesty and beauty in them, we behold the Master who is the embodiment of that beauty and majesty.

To see the Master in his truth, you have to come out from the dark curtain of your past.

My life must turn round the axis of dedication to the Master and all the truth which he represents and embodies.

We can know the Master only through his presence in ourselves; and we feel his nature only as our nature corresponds with his.

The Master has work for all who share his impersonal purpose.   He is not only a reservoir of force, a fountain of spiritual wisdom, but also an intelligence that guides.

To know him truly, you must love him and know him in all beings.

The Master unites the being of the pupil with his own, and the energy that flows forth is a pure energy which the pupil uses to change himself, a change which involves the harmonization of all his principles into a state of integral functioning.

Let us learn to look at all things as the Master looks at them, lift our hearts and eyes to the mountain-top where he dwells, to the heights where the air is serene and pure, and where it is possible to catch the first rays of the rising sun, which are those ideas that filter into our twilight world from the reservoir of Divine Thought.

Loyalty to the Master means loyalty to the Truth he embodies and the duty we owe to him who brings the Truth to us.

In the Adepts the perfection of all-round development is evident. They are extremely practical and business-like on the one side, economizing every ounce of force and using it to the best advantage, but They are also refined with an exquisiteness and finish of manner, which is truly aristocratic. Their refinement is not artificial, but natural. Just as a flower is a finished product of Nature in the plant stage, so is the Adept in the human.

Spread before him the prayer carpet of your humility.

Discover that to which you can make a complete surrender of yourself. That is the Master; that is the Truth.

We cannot know the Master until we become one with him. Where we are beautiful, there we are at one with him; his being is expressed through ours.

When I want something for myself, I have forgotten him; when I have forgotten myself, I remember him.

One can be taught in silence, the Master can communicate inwardly; there can be the circulation of life-currents between him and the one who has entered the globe of his influence, as there is between a mother and the child enfolded in her.

The Master to whom we look up ought not to be a mere name or image, but he should be an ever more beautiful Reality. In terms of our experience, which is the reality for us relatively speaking, he is the ideal, the *ne plus ultra* of our present realization, the embodiment of all that is most exquisite to our imagination. He represents the conception which each of us has of the human or spiritual perfection which we hope one day to attain.

On that harp which is the Master, any wandering breeze can but produce sweet music.

Imagine how he lives, knowing that our noblest imaginings can but touch the fringe of his reality. Yet do not be afraid, do not seek to keep up appearances; plunge in and try.

The Master is the star of our aspirations. That star will grow in brightness and power as we gaze upon it and orient every movement of our lives to its place therein.

It is in the silence of a wholly self-forgetful life that the voice of the true Master is heard, and it is heard in the background of melody which portrays the truth about ourselves.

The Master is the sum of all true ideals. His life is a current that flows into the heart and makes it feel as nothing in itself, yet capable of all things by virtue of his spiritual presence.

He draws me onward, fulfils and completes me. May I so utterly surrender myself at all times to his Light, that my life may be in constant flower with his purpose.

Let me have no other aim than Nature's aim; no other plan than the plan of God; no other love but love of man; no other will than the will of Eternity.